Copyright © 2021, by Gene Festa

All rights reserved.

No part of this book may be reproduced or transmitted in any form or by any means, electronic or mechanical, including photocopying, recording, or by any information storage and retrieval system, without permission in writing from the copyright owner.

To order additional copies of this book, contact:

Pineal Press
247 Commercial St. NE
Salem, OR 97301

http://pinealpress.com
orders@pinealpress.com

ISBN:	Hardcover	978-1-956845-03-7
	Softcover	978-1-956845-04-4
	e-Book	978-1-956845-05-1

Library of Congress Control Number: 1-956845-03-8
Print information available on last page

Rev. Date: 02/22/2022

Edition: 10 9 8 7 6 5 4 3 2 **1**

OPENING THE DOOR

Lessons of Life:
Shared and Learned

Gene Festa

✌ TABLE OF CONTENTS ✌

		SHARED	LEARNED
p. 8	1.	Domenica Anne Festa	Love of Life
p. 10	2.	Eugene A. Festa, Sr.	Being a True 'Gentle Man'
p. 13	3.	Donna Festa Hintersehr	Steadfastness
p. 15	4.	James Paul Festa	A Good Heart
p. 18	5.	Michelle Lynne Dowell	Becoming a Gift for Others
p. 20	6.	Nicholas & Isabella Dowell	Finding The Child Within
p. 23	7.	Suzanne Marion	Serenity
p. 25	8.	Harry Hennes	Serving Others
p. 27	9.	Pablo Sicilia	Love of the Marginalized
p. 30	10.	My Students	Being a Lifelong Learner
p. 32	11.	My Catholic Church	Living With Ambiguity
p. 35	12.	Hurricane Ike, Sept. 2008	Take Nothing for Granted
p. 38	13.	Francis Bok	Surviving Life's Curveballs
p. 41	14.	The Holocaust	History as a Teacher
p. 43	15.	John Cooper	Taking Risks
p. 45	16.	Georgia & Eddie Leonard	Dedication
p. 47	17.	Cheryl, Gary, & Others	Collegiality
p. 49	18.	Newfoundland	A Spirit of Adventure
p. 52	19.	Holocaust Survivors	Hope
p. 54	20.	Jagdish Davè	True Happiness in Life
p. 56	21.	September 11, 2001	Bravery and Sacrifice
p. 58	22.	Oprah W., Sam S., & Jesus	Learning to Say Thank You
p. 61	23.	The Gaetas	The Importance of Family
p. 64	24.	Mother Teresa	True Love of Others
p. 66	25.	Oscar Romero	Standing Up for Justice
p. 69	26.	John "Jack" Carr	Being a Great Teacher
p. 72	27.	Elizabeth "Bette" Breaz	True Friendship
p. 75	28.	The Indispensable Man	Taking Life Too Seriously
p. 78	29.	Rev. Dr. Martin L. King, Jr.	Dreaming Your Dream
p. 81	30.	St. Francis of Assisi	Priorities
p. 83	31.	Catholic Relief Services	Faith In Action
p. 85	32.	All Those Not Mentioned	Appreciating Life's Gifts

~ PROLOGUE ~

In April of 1968 I had just graduated from college, and was reclassified 1A by my draft board, in preparation for Vietnam. I moved home to my parent's house to await my fate. Getting restless, and needing some money, I began to substitute teach and found that I enjoyed it. About the same time, in April of that year, Martin Luther King was assassinated in Memphis.

I remember it well. Mobs ran into the streets, destroying buildings, looting, and setting fire to business, as well as homes... all in desperation and incredulity. Washington, DC, near my parents' home in Maryland was soon ablaze, just a day after that terrible event. It was a Friday.

On Palm Sunday, I went to my family's church and heard the local priest put out a plea for volunteers to go around that afternoon to the neighborhoods, and collect food for people who were now homeless and without anything to sustain them. Why not, I thought. I had never done anything like that, and it sounded like something I could easily do.

That afternoon has stayed with me. I walked around, knocking on doors and begging for food. What I remember clearly is having many doors slammed in my face, being yelled and cursed at, and hearing all types of names for those who were in the cities rioting. I was quickly discouraged, because in my innocence and naiveté, I truly believed people would immediately seize on this opportunity to help their less fortunate brothers and sisters. I was in for a rude awakening.

After a couple of discouraging hours, I started up the walk of yet another neatly kept house, and knocked on the door. It was answered by a man who was barefoot, wearing jeans and a t-shirt. He was holding a crying child in one hand, and a bottle in the other. This young father was clearly home alone that Sunday afternoon, taking care of his infant child. I could sense his frustration as I gave him my spiel, fully expecting to have another door slammed in my face. What happened first was a surprise to me, and second, something I have never forgotten. It was a defining moment in my young life.

The young father, instead of telling me to get out, etc., said nothing to me except, "Follow me". He walked into the house, through the kitchen and stopped next to a door. With his foot, he opened the door of the pantry, filled with shelves of food, then looked at me and said, "Help yourself... take whatever you want". Then, he continued into the living room to continue feeding his child.

Frankly, I was shocked. This was such a contrast to how I had been treated all afternoon. I filled a bag, offered my thanks, and left. I thought about that brief scene... a lot.

That young father, even in *his* need, took the time to share what he had with others. Others he did not know or have any connection with. Yet, he did reach out, and he taught me a valuable lesson: in this life, we are to make a difference by sharing what is inside of *our* pantry... to give of ourselves in many ways. That simple act of kindness compelled me to begin formulating my own philosophy of life.

I believe in being proactive, and making things happen for the better, and came to the decision that I will strive to leave the world a better place than before I passed through.

As you will come to see, my greatest passion in life is peace and justice for all. However, that cannot happen if we are self-centered and inward thinking. It is only when we see the true value of others, and relate to them in positive and affirming ways, that we can genuinely make a difference.

In my life, I have come to realize that scores of folks have done just that for me. I believe in what I do and am the kind of man I am, because of all I have learned and been given by others. Many events and places have influenced me, and the people along the way have willingly opened their "pantries", and invited me to share in what they could give.

This collection of stories is my offering to you. Within these pages are the lessons of life others have shared with me, and which, in most cases, I continue to pass on. These are the interests, passions, blessings, lessons, and qualities that others have passed on to me, in as generous a way as that young father did on Palm Sunday, 1968. To this day, I still do not know his name, but I will never forget him, nor the many others mentioned in these pages. I dedicate this book to this unknown teacher of mine and to all the other people places and events, mentioned or not here in this book, that have made me who I am today.

What I offer is the proverbial "tip of the iceberg", as they say. The people who headline each chapter are not the only players who have made an appearance on the stage of this man's life. There are scores more who have influenced and offered me so much, whom may or may not be mentioned, but am grateful to, nonetheless.

Each vignette will be brief, followed by a section I call "Going Further"... Here you will find questions to ponder and suggested activities to experience more of each chapter's particular topic.

As I enjoy retirement and the twilight years of a life well lived, I present this wisdom as a gift to you, the reader.

Enjoy!

CHAPTER 1

"Love of Life"
Domenica Anne Festa, My Mother

My mom was likely born on a Sunday, as that is what her first name means in Italian. She came from a rather large family of Italian immigrants who settled in Westchester County, New York.

She married my dad in 1944, when he was on leave from his duties in the Army. Soon after, he shipped out to Europe. A few months later I was born. Apparently, my mom had a hard delivery, as I have always been told the doctor had to use forceps. This left my face pretty marked up, and caused a large bump to develop, which later grew. I was also told that if it had gone inward, I most likely would have died. My mom often told me she considered me a miracle child, because I did survive, and the bump gradually went away.

My earliest memories of my mother are good. I remember a fun, loving, happy person who loved to sing. In fact, I am sure that I inherited the "singing gene" from her. She sang to us a lot, and was part of a singing group once. She had a beautiful voice, and I enjoyed listening to her.

My aunts told me when she was growing up, she sang a lot. In fact, there were several young ladies from her church (the "Italian" church in town), including my mom who were often asked to sing at weddings and funerals. She told me she liked that, since she could get out of school for weekday morning funerals!

My mom was affectionate and loving and often hugged us. She doted on her boys (just ask my sister!), and what I remember most is her total enjoyment of life. She instilled in me a real love of life in general, and an attitude of believing in the "cup half full."

Like any emotional Italians, she yelled a lot. I mean, *a lot*. But, no matter what, I always felt that she loved us kids and would do anything for us. Others saw that in her too.

She was an Air Force officer's wife and assumed that role well, being active in many activities on the Base, no matter where we were. She was active in the church choir, as well as volunteer projects in the community. In fact, I remember a reporter wrote an article about her willingness to help others. It was titled, "Dial 'M' for Maggie". Everyone called her Maggie. Why? I never found out, but I still have a copy of that article.

My mom was full of life. I was devastated when she suddenly died of a cerebral hemorrhage at age 46, just two days before my 19th birthday. I could not believe it, and was angry. Angry at everyone, but most especially, God. Eventually, through the help of others, I got over it, but I truly missed her and her smiling presence. She filled a room with joy and laughter, and the absence of that has, to this day, been hard to accept.

But, in all the losses of my life, I have always tried to learn and move on. There have been many times I regretted her not being able to meet her granddaughter who, like her, has an incredible love of life and song. Sadly, I look at my grandchildren and realize how much fun they would have had with her. But, the memory of her, and her great love of life, fills me with joy and hope, and a positive attitude to enjoy every day of my life to the fullest. This has been my mom's wonderful gift to me.

Going Further…

1. What "mother figures" have graced your life?

2. What gives you "joy" in life?

3. What is your life's "theme song?"

CHAPTER 2

"Being a True 'Gentle Man'"
Eugene A. Festa, Sr., My Dad

It was only after my father's death in September, 1998, that I began to fully grasp how wonderful a human being he was. At his wake service, I remember standing at the foot of his casket, receiving guests who had come to pay their respects. One after another, they came to shake my hand and tell me how much they respected my father and how much he had done for them. For several hours, I stood there and greeted person after person. So many people came to pay their respects! As I reflected on his life, I realized what a great role model he was for me.

A model of a good father and husband, a model of a good manager and boss, and an excellent grandfather. As I recall in my time growing up, I remember my dad as being a kind and considerate man, who knew when and how to be strict (very strict at times when we needed it), yet also how to be gentle and loving. If you were to ask his granddaughters (the older ones who had a chance to know him), they would tell you how much they loved their "Pop".

He showed me how to be a man who could command respect and attention from his men (he was a career Air Force officer), and at the same time be a loving, devoted family man; not afraid to take time to play with his kids, sing songs with them, and tell them stories.

His subordinates respected him, which I could see when I spent time at his office. The young airmen under his command, often away from home for the first time, looked to him for advice and help... and he willingly gave it to them. His patience and caring always impressed me, though I can also remember being the recipient of strict punishments when I did something wrong!

Although he was never a violent person, we knew that we had to toe the line. He expected us to be good, and study hard. Although he never went to college, his success came from hard work and applied effort, and those values were instilled in us.

When I graduated from college, he wanted me to work in Washington, DC, and helped me get a job. After a few months I was awarded a scholarship, which allowed me to go to graduate school. Two years later, I decided not to return to government work, but instead to begin teaching. One of the biggest shocks for me came the day I finally landed my first teaching job, after more than 6 months of intense job searching and interviews. I excitedly called my dad to let him know, and his only comment was, "Is that all you could get?" I was devastated, but still pursued my dream of teaching. A few years later, when I won my first teaching award, and again called my dad to tell him, he quietly and thoughtfully made a remark which told me he did understand my passion for teaching: "So, you really do want to do this teaching thing I guess." From then on, I would often hear him tell people that his son was a teacher, and a good one at that!

My dad taught me a lot, but mostly I remember him for the gentleness and love he showed people. It reminded me that a real man can, indeed, show that side of himself and never fear to lose anything of what he is. In fact, he becomes a better man when he touches people with love. This is what those many mourners meant when they lined up to tell me that my dad meant so much to them. I truly believe he had no enemies in his well lived life, only people whom he touched, and who remembered him as a truly "gentle man."

Before he died, dad was very ill. Only 3 months before, he had a quintuple bypass surgery at age 80... from which he never really recovered. I was happy to be able to travel cross-country to spend a couple weeks with him that summer, and to this day, I will always remember the last time I saw him. As I hugged him good-bye, we both said "I love you". I knew I would never see him again, and yet I knew that we had been able to express our love for one another. I had no regrets. I was proud to have been named after him, and to share those qualities which he passed on to me.

Going further…

1. What memories do you have of your Dad?

2. Who in your life has shown you gentleness and compassion?

3. What lesson would you like to leave your children one day?

CHAPTER 3

"Steadfastness"
Donna Festa Hintersehr, My Sister

My sister Donna and I were born 14 months apart. From my earliest recollections, I can say we have been best friends ever since. We grew up together, and were inseparable. That meant we got into trouble a lot together! But we were always there for each other. In fact, many considered us twins!

Donna was always "bossy"... I mean that in a good way. She was always a take charge type of person, and often organized the games and activities for us. We looked to her often for guidance and direction, and could always be depended on from our childhood to this very day.

As I look back, I realize that Donna has been more than just a sibling. She has truly been the "glue" which kept our family going, especially after the sudden death of our mom.

Donna was only 2 weeks away from her high school graduation when our mom suddenly passed. From that moment on, she was called upon to take on much more responsibility than many her age. Since I was away in college, she had to take on the role of running the house for our father and younger brother, who was still in grade school. I don't think I will ever be able to express to her, my feelings of appreciation for what she did at that terrible time in our lives.

Donna has exhibited great determination and organization all her life, and this has carried over to all of us. This shows through in whatever she takes on...whether it is being a good wife for her dear husband, Steve; a great mom for her wonderful girls, my nieces Stephanie and Karen; and now as a proud "Nona" to her granddaughters, Angelina, Claire, Molly, and Maddie. As she has been all of her life, Donna is there now, for her own daughters, as they have grown into motherhood.

Like many others in my life, Donna has given me so much and taught me a lot. She has given of herself for many, and I can say without a doubt, that she has definitely been an important part of our family.

Going Further...

1. What memories do you have of your siblings?

2. Who, or what, has provided the "glue" to keep *your* family together?

CHAPTER 4

"A Good Heart"
James Paul Festa, My Little Brother

On Thanksgiving Day, 1955, my grandmother put the turkey in the oven, and as it cooked, my dad, sister, and I left for the hospital. We were going to pick up my mom and our new baby brother, who was born a few days before. James Paul Festa was ten years younger than me, which meant that as he grew, I was a mean older brother.

I picked on him, made his life miserable, and yet, he never truly hated me. He was always nice to me, followed me around of course, and in general, accepted whatever I dished out to him.

His birth was significant for all of us. My sister and I had grown up as a team... and now, here was this upstart!

My sister ended up being the #1 babysitter, and as Jimmy grew, she was put in charge of him more and more. As we became teenagers, and Jimmy started school, my sister was almost his second mom. When our mom suddenly died, she truly became his surrogate mother.

I always wondered just how much my mom's death impacted Jimmy. He was the one who found her lying on the bathroom floor that day when he came home from school. Being only 19, I could not or was not able to actually sit and talk with him about that day. I know he talked with my aunts, and then chose to be rather silent about it. I always felt he was cheated in some way. Only eight years old and without a mom.

Luckily, my dad found someone wonderful and eventually married her. Maria Theresa became our stepmother, and has been, to this day, such an important part of our lives. Our half-sister, Tina came along, and Jimmy was able to grow up in a more "normal" family. "Mari", as we call called her, proved to be a loving, caring mother for all of us, especially Jimmy.

Jimmy was always a good person. He had his moments of being selfish and self-centered, as he grew up. We attributed that to the fact that, in our opinion, he was "spoiled". But Jimmy always had a big heart, and a great capacity to love others. This was obvious when he became an uncle, and our girls absolutely idolized him. Whenever they were with him, they knew that he loved each one of them with an unconditional abandon. They placed him on a pedestal from their earliest days of knowing him.

Those that knew him felt the same way, and Jimmy had many, many friends. When he was about 30, we found to our dismay that he was HIV+. He suffered with that horrible disease until his death in 1992, two weeks before his 37th birthday. I know that he most likely contracted that disease from some irresponsible behavior, but I never turned away from him, nor did I judge him. Throughout his illness, he was upbeat and cheerful, and taught us a lot about life, and how precious it is. He lived every moment he could, as happily and positively as possible.

At the time of his death, he was employed by the City Opera of New York as its company manager. I will never forget his memorial service. Who else can say that soloists from the Opera, the Gay Men's Chorus of NYC, and a prominent church in the Village came to sing at their funeral? Jim's passion was singing, which he shared with others, bringing much joy into their lives. His death left a real void in our hearts and lives, but he taught us one big lesson: bring as much joy into peoples' lives as possible, by truly showing them what it means to be a good person. From this great loss in our lives, we learned to look up, each of us becoming more knowledgeable about AIDS, and I decided to become an AIDS educator and volunteer.

My little brother taught us so much, and was a gift to others and me. I have missed him, and all he could have continued to give us.

Going Further...

1. What does "goodness" mean to you?

2. What song speaks to your heart? Why?

3. I recommend *7 Days at the Hot Corner*, by Terry Trueman. This is a great piece of young adult fiction, and while it does not totally center of the topic of AIDS, the disease does play a part in the overall story. I was especially touched by something the author says near the end of the book, on pp. 138-39:

"...AIDS or no AIDS, life is about the way you live, how you treat the people you love. It really is about how you play the game."

❧ CHAPTER 5 ❦

"Becoming a Gift for Others"
Michelle Lynne Festa Dowell, My Daughter

My daughter was born on a cold winter's afternoon, in December of 1973, in Annapolis, MD. From the moment I set eyes on her, I was proud to be her dad, and felt a tremendous amount of love for her.

We had not yet decided on a girl's name when we left for the hospital that day, but somehow, we came up with "Michelle Lynne". Little did we know how significant that name choice would be! We found out her names meant "beautiful gift of God", and I can say that throughout her life, she has been just that… a beautiful gift for us and others.

Michelle was always a loving and caring person growing up, and she has continued to be that way. She loves music, probably because she and I sang together from an early age. I would play the guitar, and she would sing. I was not surprised that after many years of singing in choirs and performing on stage, she decided to major in voice in college.

That was a hard thing for me to take. I knew she most likely would not follow that career path, but I wanted her to find that out for herself. Perhaps, it was a bit costly in the long run, but that was her choice to make. After graduation, she decided to enter an alternative certification program to become a teacher. Not just a teacher, however, a special education teacher.

For many years she has been sharing her wonderful gifts with pre-school children who have a need for the special kind of time and care that she is able to provide. She is truly a gift to them, as she has been to her dear family, and me over the years. She exhibits great patience and understanding when working with special needs children and their families, along with great insight, and perception. She is often sought out for advice. I have been most honored and proud to see her follow in the same profession as mine, but even more so to see the absolute good she has accomplished.

Michelle is a good wife and mother, and works hard to provide a good home for her family. I have always been proud of her, and anyone who knows me can speak to that fact. I count raising my daughter as a single dad, as one of my greatest accomplishments. Her mom and I divorced when she was almost 9, and she lived with me during much of the school year. That made me appreciate even more the unique gift that is Michelle. She taught me to look everyone who come into our lives as precious gifts, to be appreciated and esteemed.

My daughter never lets me forget how much I mean to her, and I must say, some of the most beautiful greeting cards I have ever seen, have come from her on my birthday, holidays, or special events. On her wedding day, I made it a point to be brave and not cry (too much!). I could not have been more proud of her, and was honored to be able to walk her down the aisle and perform the ceremony. It was then, that I realized that no matter what she did, nor with whom she lived, she would always, truly, be God's beautiful gift to me.

Going Further...

1. Who or what has been your beautiful gift from God?

2. How have you been a gift for others?

CHAPTER 6

"Finding The Child Within"
Nicholas Aiden Dowell & Isabella Grace Dowell
My Grandchildren

"In every real man a child is hidden that wants to play."
(Friedrich Wilhelm Nietzsche, Philosopher)

I met Nicholas Dowell in San Antonio after meeting his father, Nathan, who had been dating my daughter. Nicholas was in diapers, just a year old. We seemed to be friends from the minute we met.

As my daughter and Nathan became more involved, I got to know Nicholas better. The next year, they all came to my home in Houston for Christmas. A few days later, we all drove back to San Antonio, in a caravan, so to speak. When we had to make a "pit stop" for my daughter Michelle's dog, Cadence, we all wandered around a roadside rest stop. At the time, Nathan was still being polite and calling me "Mr. Festa".

As we were getting ready to leave, Nathan called over to me. Nicholas perked up his ears and repeated what he had heard… "Festa". From that moment on, I became "Festa" to Nicholas, and it is what he calls me to this day.

He has come to understand what a grandfather is, but still calls me by his special name. Our relationship has been important, since Nathan's father is no longer with us. I definitely became Nicholas's grandfather. I love him, and he loves me.

Nicholas and I have a great time playing together. I have fished with him, played miniature golf, basketball, and bowled. We have gone swimming, to zoos and amusement parks, and spent special time at many playgrounds together. We have played computer games, watched movies, and even cooked dinner for his parents. We enjoy each other's company, and though he is older now and the times are not as numerous, I will certainly treasure those times. Nicholas has shared with me a most precious gift: how to be a child. He has shown me how wonderful it is to forget trying to impress anyone, and to just be myself.

Isabella Dowell came into my life only a short time ago. In March, 2009, when she was born, her big brother was already 7. Just moments after her birth, when I first laid eyes on her, I realized that she, like her brother, would forever be the light of my life. In her short time with us, she has brought me so much happiness. As a baby, when she looked up at me and smiled, or made cooing sounds, my heart soared.

I was so happy to retire and move to San Antonio. It has allowed me and Isabella to share countless hours and activities together. I have read her stories, had tea parties, and taken long walks to share special grandpa and granddaughter secrets. We have visited museums, watched movies, taken road trips, and shared countless other precious moments together. Unlike Nicholas, her name for me has never been "Festa". Long before she was born, he and I decided that this would be a name just for him to call me. For Isabella, I am "Papa". This is her special name for me, and as she grows older, we have become even closer. Spending time with Bella is truly a blessing for me.

Isabella and Nicholas represent every child in my life, and there have been many in my 30+ years of teaching. My students, like my grandchildren, showed me the value of searching deep within, for the little boy or girl in all of us. They taught me the beauty of innocence, and honesty…the "what you see is what you get" part of my life. I am truly grateful to all of them for allowing me to do this.

In short, Nicholas and Isabella have not only been my grandchildren, but also my buddies. We have spent a lot of time together, and, like my students, I was always learning something from them. I consider myself a lifelong learner, and the children in my life have taught me the most about appreciating the gift of living. Nicholas and Bella, as many others, have been the true teachers in my life!

Going Further…

1. Who calls forth the child in YOU?

2. What lesson would you want to leave to a child who means a lot to you?

CHAPTER 7

"Serenity"
Suzanne Marion, My Friend and Music Teacher

I have known Suzie Marion since the early 1990's. We met through a mutual friend who studied piano with her. It was the year my daughter left for college, and I realized that I would no longer have to pay for her music lessons. That's when I decided to pursue a lifelong dream: learn to play the piano. I got Suzie's phone number and called her.

Imagine my surprise when she told me she had no room for me. She was fully booked with students. I insisted, and eventually talked her into taking me on Saturday mornings, at a time she gave up just for me! I started my piano lessons, and a wonderful friendship developed.

Five years later, I also started voice lessons with Suzie. When she challenged me to sing in my first recital, I dropped piano. I didn't mind, since the piano was much more difficult than singing! Since then, I have sung in more concerts, recitals, and benefits than I can count. Each time, it has been with the encouragement of this positive influence in my life.

I can now sing in 7 languages, thanks in great part to Suzie's encouragement. She never discouraged me when I wanted to do something, and was willing to work with me until I "got it." She has many wonderful qualities: great wife and mother, a good and faithful friend to many people, talented musician and singer, and a wit and intellect to rival many. What really stands out to me when I think of her is the great serenity in her personality.

I have seen Suzie face many challenges, with her family and extended family, including her husband Stu's health problems, as well as preparing for and taking part in many performances. She is always calm (at least on the outside) and so serene, and passes that serenity on to whomever is around her.

Suzie loves to read, study Spanish, write, and exercise. She has even published a couple children's books. This is her way of relaxing which contributes to the wonderful personality she so willingly shares with everyone. She is a friend who is always there for others, and never hesitates to volunteer to help out with any project. I cannot begin to guess how many benefits and causes she has had a hand in.

Her many years in the Houston music community have produced countless musician friends and singers that she can call on whenever there is a need, and she does! No one hesitates to help her, knowing she is always the first to be there for us, with her smile and calm demeanor. Yes, she often brings many things to many people, but it is her gift of serenity which is truly impressive. Most people will agree that knowing her, and being around her, makes them a better person. If she ever truly retires, which I doubt she will, this will be the greatest legacy she could leave for all of us.

Going Further...

1. Read and ponder the words of what is known as "The Serenity Prayer." For me, this perfectly describes my friend Suzie's outlook on life.

    God grant me the COURAGE to change the things I can change, the SERENITY to accept those I cannot change, and the WISDOM to know the difference. But God, grant me the courage not to give up on what I think is right, even though I think it is hopeless.

❧ CHAPTER 8 ☙

"Serving Others"
My good friend, Harry Hennes

"My father always used to say that when you die, if you've got five real friends, then you've had a great life."
(Lee Iacocca, Auto Executive)

I am a lucky man. Though not wealthy in terms of money, I am rich. My wealth has to do with the many friends I have been blessed with in my life. Harry Hennes is one of the best.

I met Harold S. Hennes the day I entered the Pontifical College Josephinum in the 9th grade. We both attended this seminary, ostensibly to become a priest one day, so many years ago. Neither of us stayed the 12 years to get ordained as a priest, but we began a friendship that has lasted to this day.

From that first moment we met, I knew Harry was a special person. Whomever Harry meets becomes his friend. He is one of the most generous and loving people I have ever known.

Many years later, as we looked at a picture of our class taken that first week we met, we noticed an interesting fact: Harry and I were standing next to each other in the group. We must have become instant friends then, and have continued into our senior years and retirement.

What I remember most about Harry is his willingness to lend a helping hand anytime, to anyone, with anything that needed to be done. He was as kind as he was generous and people respected him. Over the years, he taught me a lot about the value of serving others, and being selfless, which has continued into his adult years. For example, he once told me, that when a blizzard would hit northern Ohio where he lives, he would often go out with his snow blower and not only to clear his driveway and sidewalk, but also the entire street. He will often drive several hours to help his friends and neighbors, as well as his relatives.

I was once the recipient of Harry's aid, when my mom died. It was sudden, and we were in college. I had to leave, barely having time to pack. To this day, I will never forget how wonderful he made me feel, when upon my return he told me he had stripped my bed, washed the sheets, remade the bed, did my laundry, and cleaned my room. I was so struck with his attitude of serving others, that I have never forgotten it. I often hearken back to that memory, as I try to do the same for others.

I wish more people had an attitude like Harry's. I wish more people would reach out to their neighbor to simply lend a helping hand, as my buddy, Harry has always done. In the book *Servant Leadership*, Kent M. Keith speaks of this type of attitude in the business world, which can easily be seen as a real possibility in everyday life. He says " How much better a world would we be living in if more people had the attitude of reaching out to others, unselfishly and compassionately," just as Harry does. In addition to being a great husband, father, and teacher, Harry Hennes has also been, a great friend and role model for me.

Going Further…

1. Think about this quote from Robert Greenfield's seminal essay, "The Servant as Leader":

    *"The servant leader **is** servant first. It begins with the natural feeling that one wants to serve, to serve **first**. A servant leader is simply **a leader who is focused on serving others**."* [1]

    What does this mean to you?

2. Think about the last time you reached out to serve someone.

---

[1] *The Case for Servant Leadership,* by Kent M. Keith, pp. 1 and 9

CHAPTER 9

"Love of the Marginalized"
Fr. Pablo Sicilia, My First Spanish Teacher

Fr. Paul Sicilia was not a priest when I first met him. He taught us religion while in his last year of seminary and I was a freshman in high school. Following his ordination in May 1960, he went to Mexico to study Spanish and returned to teach at the seminary where I was a student.

He started a Spanish language program, which would one day become an incredible part of the curriculum there, as well as an important part of the seminary life. We were his first class and, I'm afraid we would never let him forget it.

We were horrible to him, and he would often get frustrated and chew us out. Yet, we soon began to see his total dedication to this language and somehow, we all began to love it as much as he did.

I believe we came to that conclusion, because we saw that Pablo used his Spanish language skills to minister to the Mexican migrant workers in northern Ohio at that time. He often left the seminary near Columbus, Ohio after classes on Friday afternoons, and drove several hours north to where several migrant workers labored in the fields. He spent many weekends ministering to them, and often returned early Monday morning, running in at the last minute to teach our class. He would recount everything he had done that weekend, and filled us with his enthusiasm and love for the workers. It was during that time I learned many Spanish songs, which I would eventually sing with many students over the years when, due to Pablo's influence, I decided to become a Spanish teacher.

I soon learned that this humble, giving man was dedicated to helping and loving people who were somehow on the edge of society. He reached out to the unfortunate and needy without thinking of himself, and became a role model to me, and a real example of what it means to serve others.

Pablo defined the word ministry, and later in life, I think of him fondly and remember what I learned from him.

He was a priest who loved what he did. He was dedicated and unselfish in reaching out to those whom he served, and continued serving after he left teaching to became a parish priest. Always humble, I remember his refusing to accept the honor of being named a monsignor, until his archbishop ordered him to do so.

After Pablo retired, we kept in touch. Although it was difficult for him to retire, he continued to enjoy his favorite pastime: traveling the world. It seemed he knew someone everywhere he went with "family" on every continent. He served as a minister on cruise ships, and when he was not travelling, he spent hours visiting the sick in hospitals and ministering in prisons.

In the days of clerical abuse in the Catholic Church, Rev. Pablo Sicilia has stood out for me as a true example of what a good, loving priest is, and should be. This example has been another one of the great gifts people in my life have given to me. Pablo died suddenly one night in August 2009. It was a loss to the many he served, and a real personal loss to me. I was glad to visit him in San Antonio where he lived, to introduce him to my new granddaughter, Bella, a month before he passed. I still think of him often, especially when preparing to preach or minister in some other way.

Going Further...

Here is one of the Spanish songs Pablo taught us on one of those Mondays, after returning from ministering to the migrant field workers. It is a favorite of mine, which I sang often with my Spanish classes.

"De Colores" is a well-known traditional folk-song in the Spanish-speaking world. The song was brought to the Americas from Spain during the 16th century. In modern times, this song frequently appears in collections of children's songs. It has been an unofficial anthem for the United Farm Workers union.

The words of the song are an expression of joy and a celebration of all creation with its many bright colors. The two verses listed below are the most commonly used. Look for it on YouTube to sing along!

De colores… De colores se visten los campos en la primavera
De colores… De colores son los pajaritos que vienen de afuera
De colores… De colores es el arco iris que vemos lucir
Y por eso los grandes amores de muchos colores me gustan a mí
Y por eso los grandes amores de muchos colores me gustan a mí

Colorful, colorful are the little birds that come from far away
Colorful, colorful is the rainbow that we see shining
And that is why I like wonderful colorful things
And that is why I like wonderful colorful things

Canta el gallo… Canta el gallo con el kiri kiri kiri kiri kiri
La gallina… La gallina con el cara cara cara cara cara
Los pollitos… Los pollitos con el pío pío pío pío pío pí
Y por eso los grandes amores de muchos colores me gustan a mí
Y por eso los grandes amores de muchos colores me gustan a mí

The rooster sings, the rooster with a kiri kiri quiri kiri kiri
The hen sings, the hen with a cluck cluck cluck cluck cluck
The chicks, the chicks with a peo peo peo peo pi
And that is why I like wonderful colorful things
And that is why I like wonderful colorful things

~ CHAPTER 10 ~

"Becoming a Lifelong Learner"
All My Students, in 34 Years of Teaching

Over the 30+ years I was in education, I suppose thousands of young minds entered my life. Many are memorable; others, I truly do not remember. Some have become and remained good friends. Some I remember for the terrible times we spent together; others I remember more for all they gave me. Mentioning some by name will surely offend others, so I choose not to. If one of you is reading this, know that you have somehow impacted me in my tenure as a teacher. You touched me and I became a different, better person.

One thing my students taught me from day one, in September of 1970, was to never stop being open minded and flexible. They taught me that life is not always perfect, and there is always room for improvement. And very importantly, they taught me to look for new things to learn each and every day. The columnist Frank A. Clark said, "Every adult needs a child to teach; it's the way adults learn." I have been fortunate in my life to have had so many excellent teachers as good role models. I always had one goal: to learn something from my students every day. I decided long ago when the day came that I was not learning any more, then I would finally retire. Happily, that day never came. To this day, I felt my students gave me as much or more than I gave them.

For example, early in my teaching career, I learned the value of patience. I was not patient when I first ventured into a classroom, but I soon learned that if I was ever going to reach my students, I must force myself to count to 10 (even 20!) and give them a chance. I have always been grateful for that gift. I also learned from the start the need to be compassionate and loving. It was expected and needed by the students, and it taught me to be that way. The most important gift my students have given me is to remember the child in me. The philosopher Friedrich Wilhelm Nietzsche once said: "In every real man a child is hidden that wants to play." In order to relate to my students and reach them (no matter their age), I have never forgotten the value of play. This, I believe, has served me well, and I am truly grateful to my students for helping me to remember that.

I believe teaching is one of the most noble of all professions, and I have never regretted my choice to become a teacher. For a few years, I left education and briefly worked in business, but I was miserable. I returned to teaching, as luck would have it, at the same school I had left, and I was re-energized! If I have any regrets, it is perhaps that I was not the teacher I should have been for some students, but I will never know that. The positive side has been the feedback from many students and their families, coupled with several awards, that tells me that my job was well worth the effort and persistence. The rewards were not monetary, but much more lasting and valuable. My students' reactions and life lessons have made it all worthwhile.

Going Further...

1. What teacher do you remember? Why?

2. Why not look that teacher up today, and if he/she is still living, write a note to them. You will make their day, trust me!

CHAPTER 11

"Living With Ambiguity"
My Catholic Church

I was baptized in the Catholic faith a month after I was born, and raised by parents who attended weekly Mass and were active in the Church. As a young man, I decided to become a priest, and entered a minor seminary in Ohio at age 14. I left 6 years later, deciding that priesthood was not for me.

That was around the time the Second Vatican Council occurred in the mid 1960's. Many changes were happening, and I loved them. I enjoyed Mass in English and singing in Church. I had begun to play the guitar and joined groups that played and sang in Church.

As a young man, I was not that active in Church. I started helping out with religion education classes after college, and when I married, it was in a Catholic Church. My wife and I moved to a small town outside of Annapolis, Maryland and were unhappy with the local congregation.

We started selling AMWAY products and luckily, one night at a meeting, we heard about a group of local Catholics. They were a type of "maverick" group that met in a Presbyterian Church on Sunday afternoons to celebrate Mass. They were known as a "non-geographic" parish, and we loved it. It was just what we wanted.

It reminded me of the first Christian communities we read about in Acts of the Apostles: small, caring, service oriented, pastoral. We remained members of the Pilgrim Community (what a name) until we moved to Texas nearly 5 years later. We literally did move, as pilgrims, to various locations to keep the community going. We had a Jesuit priest as our pastor, and had permission from the local Catholic bishop. When our daughter Michelle was born, we celebrated her Baptism within this loving and giving group.

We missed them every day after moving to Texas, but we got involved in the local parish, and liked it. Shortly after, I entered a program to become a deacon, and in 1981, I as ordained a permanent deacon.

I worked at the parish, teaching, preaching, celebrating sacraments, doing many types of pastoral work and loved it. When a new parish started close by, I was its first deacon, and stayed there for many years. I became active in the city on a diocesan level, working with youth and teaching adults. I continued taking courses, attending retreats, and generally taking part in my spiritual formation. Through all this, I have seen and felt the hand of God in my life.

As I got more involved, become more educated, taught more classes, and led many retreats, I had come to the realization just how painful it was to be a part of this Catholic Church of mine. I loved it, but it was difficult at times to reconcile within my own mind the Church I saw, and the Church I know Jesus meant us to be.

The Church I see throughout the past 2000 years has been wrought with deception and problems. Even today, I see a Church which at times is hypocritical, not allowing women their proper role, seemingly looking the other way when priests have abused children, not practicing the peace and justice that Jesus talked about so often. I have experienced priests who instead of saving souls have driven people away from faith. Today, with dismay, I see young seminarians who want to discard all the renewal and hard work of the past nearly 60 years since Vatican II, and return to a time when people were truly like sheep, always subject to the clergy and not really being a viable part of the Church. Today, I see uncertainty and disunity in this Church founded by Christ himself, which dismays me.

I love the Church of the 21st century, with its renewal and vision. I do not want to go back to the church of my childhood, when I went to Mass and understood nothing. I remember a time when lay people were not highly thought of, and took no active part in the ministerial life of this Church. I also remember a time when Scripture Study, ecumenism, and active lay participation were unheard of. I don't want to go back.

When I see folks in my Church making changes and regressing to the Church of the pre-Vatican II days, to preserve what they feel is the "real" Church, I ask, "why go backwards?" With Church attendance way down, why further alienate parishioners by trying to control them and eliminate them? I see a Church, which at times does not live the peace and justice, it preaches, and again I ask… why?

This confuses me and makes me wonder if it is all-worthwhile? As a member of the clergy, I say yes. Even though it is disconcerting, I am willing to live with the ambiguity, and to work hard to help people realize what a wonderful institution our church really is. I love it, and I do not want to give up on it. I am a true believer in this organization and will continue to work to be sure it faithfully carries on the message of its founder. I am grateful for what I have learned and received from my church. Even with its problems, it is still something I wish to hold on to. It is important to stay focused on the positives, not the negatives, as some continually do. I feel this is my calling: to hang on, and help others to do the same. This is the true calling and message of my Church.

Going Further…

1. In your life, what do you truly believe in?

2. Is there a place for "church" in our day and age? If so, what should it look like?

CHAPTER 12

"Take Nothing for Granted"
Hurricane Ike, September 2008

In the late summer of 2008, for an entire week, we were told a mighty hurricane was crossing the ocean and could possibly enter the Gulf of Mexico and head towards the Texas coast. This was not the first time meteorologists had warned us of an impending storm, and truthfully, we were fairly relaxed and blasé about it. That is, until Hurricane Ike entered the Gulf and headed towards Houston.

It looked to be a powerful storm as it churned its way across the warm waters and ravaged Cuba. As it entered the Gulf and pointed in our direction, we were told this was a very unique hurricane. It had a tremendously large center and extended hundreds of miles across. It could land anywhere from Mexico to Florida. And Houston was right in the middle of its path!

As that week progressed, Ike was heading directly to our doorstep and by Thursday, predictions had us feeling the effects. Weekend events were canceled, and schools were closed on Friday to prepare.

I had already lived through one direct hit in 1983, from Hurricane Alicia, which hit Galveston and headed right through downtown Houston. I remembered the effects of that storm, and was not looking forward to another one. Friday, September 12, 2008, dawned clear and sunny, but the wind picked up. Large waves and surges were hitting the coast, and the city of Galveston. Nearby areas were ordered to evacuate. About 75% of the people left, as the waters began to pound the coast areas. By the time I went to bed that night, it was windy and you could feel something in the air. During the night, Ike came ashore with its 75 mph winds and 90 mph hurricane blasts. I lived 50 miles from the coast, so I (mistakenly) thought it would not be too bad.

That night was one of the worst I have ever experienced. I felt my entire house shake, as the seemingly never-ending winds and rains pounded us. At one point, I wondered how sensible I was to listen to the authorities and not flee helter-skelter as we had all done some 3 years before, when another hurricane was supposed to hit us. That resulted in tremendous traffic jams and grueling road trips. I spent 6 hours on the road to make what is normally a 3-hour trip to my daughter's. There were gas shortages, food shortages, and in the end, a totally unnecessary move, since the hurricane skirted us, with not as much as a drop of rain. So, this time I had decided to "ride out the storm", as we say in hurricane prone areas.

The next day, the wind and rain continued for another 6 hours. Finally, it was calm, and I could go out to see what had happened. There was no damage to my home, but all around me looked like a battlefield. Other homes were damaged, trees and plants uprooted, and there was debris everywhere. We had no electrical power, water, phone service, nor any way to stay connected with the outside world. I had plenty of candles and one good flashlight, and a refrigerator leaking from things melting and food going bad.

When you are sitting in the dark with nothing to do, sweating from the heat and humidity, one tends to get philosophical. Hurricane Ike taught me one valuable lesson: never take anything for granted. For example, it took me an entire day to stop going into a room to turn on the light switch, only to remember there would be no light. That first night was unbearable: the heat and humidity were deathly. Early the next morning, it began to rain again, forcing me to shut the windows I had vainly opened to get some air.

As things were getting back to normal the next week, we couldn't go to work or drive on the streets. We had to live with curfews at night. The entire Island of Galveston, and other areas were devastated and destroyed. People lost everything; their entire lives whisked away by Ike. Looking at pictures of the devastation, I was reminded of movies I had seen of nuclear holocausts.

My power and water were finally restored, and life slowly returned to some semblance of normalcy. But not for thousands of Hurricane Ike victims who would be affected for the rest of their lives. Some lives were lost forever, others changed forever. And thorough it all, I came away with one valuable lesson: appreciate what I have and never take it for granted. I can't hear the name Ike without thinking of that.

Going Further…

1. Think of one thing you take for granted each day. What would your life be without it?

2. Make it a point today to call someone, or write a note to them to tell them how much you appreciate them in your life.

❧ CHAPTER 13 ❧

"Surviving Life's Curveballs"
Francis Bok

Through my volunteer work at the Houston Holocaust Museum, I heard about an incredible man, Francis Bok. He was born in the Sudan, and at the age of 7, was orphaned when his village was attacked and destroyed by Muslim militia. Both his parents were killed and Francis was kidnapped by the general of the troops who attacked his village.

For ten years, he lived as a slave to this Muslim general. His story is unbelievable, and in his published autobiography, he recounts the terrible graphic details of that day when he lost everything of importance to him in his young life, and began a life of servitude and misery.

When I first heard of Francis Bok, I was determined to contact him and attempt to bring him to my school in Houston. With luck, I did just that, and a few months later I found myself driving to the airport with two of our students to pick him up. Since Francis was nearly 7' tall, we had arranged accommodations for him in a hotel where visiting professional basketball players usually stayed when they came to town. You can imagine how I felt when I saw him come off the plane: a VERY tall black man, wearing jeans and sweat shirt, and a baseball cap on backwards. We asked him what he wanted to see, and he told us of his interest in sports. We drove him around our city to all the professional sports venues, ending up at our Holocaust Museum for a quick tour. The next day, I picked him up at the hotel so he could spend the day with us at school. Imagine my further surprise when he got off the elevator, impeccably dressed in a suit and tie.

That day was memorable. Francis was outgoing and friendly, and loved the students. He visited classes and then, after lunch, spoke at an assembly. The place was hushed, as he recounted his story of incredible cruelty and abandonment. Forced to live with animals outside, he did menial jobs for his captor and virtually lost his childhood. He was 7 when abducted and then freed by an international organization at the age of 17, ending up in Iowa. He finished high school and college, and today, he continues to work against world-wide slavery. He has spoken to the US Congress, met with presidents, and addressed university groups. His message is simple: "We must be aware of the terrible situations in the world which facilitate the enslavement of human beings, even today." He also adds: "We must work to stop this."

Francis Bok impressed us with his humility, determination, and steadfastness. We wondered, how did he end up so positive and not bitter and hateful? He lived each day looking to the future and never lost hope. A young student asked him if he celebrated his birthday while in captivity, and he told us he could not remember his own birth date. What was more mind boggling was a question from another student: "were you ever happy?" "No", he replied. He could not remember any moment of happiness during his entire captivity.

His is just one of many such stories: Holocaust victims, prisoner of war, victims of natural disasters. But all have one thing in common. As many others have done, Francis Bok impressed me with his resolute attitude and spirit of survival. He trusted in the human spirit, even as a young 7-year-old, and kept struggling to become a whole person and a free person. Maybe he didn't realize it as a youngster, but surely, he must have when he was older. Although his parents were taken from him early in his life, they gave him an incredible gift: a love of life and the will to make it through whatever he had to do, to enjoy that life.

I count meeting Francis Bok and hearing his story as a true blessing in my life.

Going Further...

1. Read the biography of Francis Bok, entitled *Escape From Slavery* (2004) ... It will surely impress you.

2. What inner strength do you draw on in times of trouble?

3. Visit **http://iabolish.com**, an American anti-slavery group, to find out what you can do to help in the struggle to end human slavery in the world.

CHAPTER 14

"History as a Teacher"
The Holocaust

"Why is history so important? Why do individuals dedicate their entire lives to a further understanding of a certain civilization or a certain government that failed miserably over three centuries ago? More importantly, why am I currently enrolled in two full year history courses at my high school. History, I believe, is one of the greatest teaching devices available to human beings. History is the ultimate test of what works and what doesn't. From the treatment of individuals, to economic systems, to law making, and ruling bodies, history offers some truly beneficial advice. History is helpful simply because we can examine how to solve problems based on how our ancestors solved, or attempted to solve, those same problems, or similar ones set in the present time."

These are the words of Rice Lummus. I met him years ago in my Spanish and Human Development (HD) classes, when he was a gangly, off-the-wall, 7th grader. Somehow, we both survived seeing each other daily, some days twice, and he managed to remember some things I taught him. He went on to major in Spanish, and remembered another important thing from HD class: he could call me by my first name when he was old enough to have a beer with me.

I have always loved history and minored in it in college. A good read for me is a great historical fiction novel. Rice wrote the above words as the introduction for his college entrance essay, which his mother later shared with me. It profoundly touched me. He went on to talk about and praise me, but what was truly impressive was this introduction about history as our teacher. His real intention was to write about how he was so moved when he took my Holocaust class in high school. For me, I saw it as a summation of why I spend so much time and effort teaching students, and being a docent to explain the horrors of the Holocaust and its profound effect on us today.

I do not dedicate myself to making people aware of this infamous time in human history just to get an emotional rise from them. It is extremely hard to talk about, and I still cry when I view photos and videos, or hear survivor stories. But I continue to do it, because in my heart I know what Rice wrote about is so true: history has a way of repeating itself, and we must learn from it to prevent certain things from ever happening again. Whether it is the Inquisition, the Fall of the Roman Empire, or the great Depression, we can look to history for answers and explanations for what is going on now. We can learn from past mistakes, as well as past successes.

I am convinced that we can live in a world of peace, if we remember the past and the mistakes made before us. Studying the causes and effects of moments like the Holocaust better prepares us to rid ourselves of hatred, and to accept everyone, thus being able to someday have a world with peace and harmony. Idealistic? Absolutely. Impossible? Perhaps. All I can do is work hard to educate and inspire others to do the same and make this world a place where my grandchildren may turn and ask their parents what the word hate means. This is why I teach and educate people of all ages.

Rice confirmed that for me in the words from an ancient Chinese proverb: "One generation plants the trees; another gets the shade."

Going Further...

1. It has been said that "a teacher affects eternity—he never knows where his influence stops". Do you agree? How has history been a teacher?

❧ CHAPTER 15 ❦

"Taking Risks"
John Cooper

I had been teaching for 5 years in 1975, and wanted a change. I decided to undertake a nationwide search for a new teaching job, and ended up in Houston, Texas to interview at a private school there.

I flew in one Saturday morning, was picked up at the airport by the principal of the high school, and driven to the home of the school's head, John Cooper. He had been the head of the Kinkaid School for nearly 25 of the school's 69 years. Handpicked by its founder, Mr. Cooper had presided over an incredible growth and expansion of the school, and was well respected and admired by the entire community.

I went through an exhaustive day of interviews, answering many questions, and seeming to talk forever. Mr. Cooper and his family lived on campus, and at the end of that busy day he invited me to take a swim in the pool, as he and his wife prepared hamburgers on the grill, and a pitcher of lemonade. We ate poolside, and then drove around that night, stopping for ice cream. The Coopers made me feel at home, introducing me to what is legendary in these parts, true Texas hospitality.

The interview continued the next day until noon, as I had to fly back home soon after. As I was leaving the school, Mr. Cooper offered me a job and handed me a contract to take home, read, and return signed. I was ecstatic! I had been searching for an entire semester, and my wife and I were weary from the process. Houston looked perfect for our small family, and I was pleased that this wonderful school had considered me a qualified candidate, and good enough to offer me a position. I have never regretted making the decision to sign that contract and move.

What I remember most about that day and what affected me greatly ever since, is Mr. Cooper's willingness to take a chance on me. He hardly knew me, but used his natural intuitiveness. I found out later, that the head of the department had been reluctant to hire me, but John chose me, nonetheless.

He was a true educator, and had spent his entire professional life in education, so, as I look back, I have to think he knew what he was doing. He was firm, but gentle in his leadership of the school, and probably had every right to pass me over. After all, I was coming from halfway across the country, with only 5 years of experience, and had actually been turned down by the school's cross-town rival. Yet, this man took a risk and gave me a chance, which I have never forgotten.

I learned a lot from that man, from the moment I met him, but what remains with me, is that every once in a while, in life, we just have to make a risky decision. I remembered that often, whether I was thinking of new and innovative ways of teaching, even changing curriculum or teaching a new course. When I have difficult personal decisions to make, with far-reaching consequences, I remember risk takers like John Cooper, and others like him. If he and others had not been willing to give me a chance, or show me how to take a risk on a relatively unknown commodity, I might never have taken the momentous step to move to a new city so far from friends and family to start a new chapter in my life. If not for him and others, I might not have made some of the important decisions which have brought me to where I am today, and made me the teacher and man I am. John Cooper taught me a valuable lesson about life: taking risks.

Going Further...

1. What does it mean to take a risk for you?

2. Think of a time when you have taken a risk. How did it turn out? What did you learn from that experience?

3. Who is a risk taker you have known or heard about?

CHAPTER 16

"Dedication"
Georgia & Eddie Leonard

I first met Georgia and Eddie Leonard when I started at the Kincaid School in 1975. They were both working in the school cafeteria. Ten years later, when management changed, Georgia and Eddie became managers of the cafeteria.

This couple were more than just workers in our cafeteria. They loved the school in every way, and dedicated themselves 100% to their work, our students, and the faculty. Everyone knew them, and they knew everyone. They called us all by name, and were thrilled when my daughter Michelle became a student at the high school. Years after Michelle left and graduated from college, they would still ask about her. That's the way they were with everyone.

They were also great cooks! The food in our cafeteria was legendary! Eddie's fried chicken was superb and a big hit each Thursday. I realize being deep fried in oil wasn't too healthy, but what a taste! In fact, one of the city papers recognized our cafeteria, and Eddie's chicken, giving it an honor that few places had received. I also loved their bread pudding, and Georgia's coleslaw. She even shared her recipe with me, and every time I make it, I think of her fondly, and enjoy it.

Georgia and Eddie were always at the school, working hard for us, and loving us. Eddie was also known by thousands of others, as the man in the blue uniform every morning and afternoon. He was out in front of the school helping kids cross the street, waving and smiling at every car that passed by. His smile and friendly greetings were an integral part of many peoples' daily commutes to and from work.

The Leonard's arrived early and stayed late. It seemed like they were always there. Deeply religious people, they spoke openly about their faith and would tell you that THEY were not in charge of what happened in life. Evenings and weekends, they were both active in their church, and always helping those less fortunate than themselves. They truly epitomized the notion of giving servants.

Georgia retired and would return once in a while to visit, telling us how every day felt like Saturday. Eddie continued to work at our cafeteria, and was even recognized by a local TV station as a Channel 2 Sunshine Award winner. The weatherman landed his helicopter on our football field one autumn morning while the entire school gathered to honor this great man (and his wife).

One day after work, Eddie did not feel well, and asked to be driven to the doctor. He died of a heart attack shortly after arriving at the doctor, which devastated all of us. We loved Eddie (and Georgia), and treasured their many years of loving dedication to all of us. The school created a special annual award for an outstanding staff member, and named it in honor of Georgia and Eddie. He was chosen as the first recipient, albeit posthumously, of the award. In 2021 Georgia died, after many happy years of retirement.

Georgia and Eddie showed all of us, with every hug and smile, what true dedication meant. They were more than an institution at our school… they defined what we all hoped to be like. I feel honored and privileged to have had them in my life, and to have learned so much from them.

Going Further…

1. To what have you been or are you dedicated? How does that show?

2. Where have you eaten the best fried chicken you've ever tasted? Who made it? What did you eat with it?

❧ CHAPTER 17 ❦

"Collegiality"
Cheryl Mitchell, Gary Klingman, & All My Fellow Teachers

I have had the privilege of working with many great colleagues, who have loved their profession and the students in their classrooms. They were dedicated professionals who gave of themselves freely.

Over the years, I have witnessed incredible generosity and dedication. These people often gave their free time to work with their students in many ways. They spent countless weekend and evening hours preparing lessons, writing reports, and gathering materials. Some have been coaches and/or club sponsors, in addition to their classroom duties. Others had double roles, taking on administrative duties in addition to their daily teaching assignments. They were always willing to share themselves, not only with their students, but with their fellow teachers.

Many times, I was on the receiving end of help and support from colleagues. They gave me encouragement and advice at times when I really needed it. Whether via informal discussions or scheduled meetings, many members of the faculties with whom I have worked, have brought me to a place of excellence in my teaching. I owe them so much, especially Cheryl Mitchell and Gary Klingman.

Cheryl and I taught 7th grade Human Development. We shared a classroom, each with our own desk and phone. Even if one of us was teaching a class, we were both comfortable with having the other one there, often taking part in their class discussions.

I enjoyed Cheryl's input, as a fellow professional, and often sought her advice. For me, she was the perfect colleague: positive, affirming, and always there to help. She was an award-winning coach and her athletes, like her students, loved her. She demanded much of them, but always had their best interests at heart. Like many of my colleagues over the years, Cheryl was a true educator: putting her students first and epitomizing the word 'professional'. She has always been positive... a true "glass half full" person who always had a smile for me. She was a good enough friend to tell me when I was wrong, and gave advice, encouragement, or pushed me when necessary. Everyone likes Cheryl.

Gary Klingman, like Cheryl, has been a colleague and one of my best friends. He and I have shared many good laughs as we worked and played together. I still remember the "nerf gun" battles we had. Gary has truly been one of the most dedicated teachers I've known in all my years in the profession. As a history teacher, he instilled in his students a true love of their country's history and traditions. Creative, and willing to take risks when it came to implementing new ideas and technology, Gary was always there for his students, and challenged them to rise to their potential. They loved him, and when he left our school to move to another city, there were many tears. We remained friends and stayed in touch. I know he continued to be the great teacher I knew him to be.

Like Cheryl Mitchell, what I admire most about Gary is his total dedication to his students... the number one quality for any effective teacher, in my eyes.

He and I were sponsors of the student council and we spent many hours involved in projects. I can honestly say that all the after-hours time and weekends with him and the students, were worth it. Gary was recognized by the city for his dedication to community service. We spent many a Saturday with groups of students and parents helping fix up older homes in distressed parts of the city. Gary has not only been a friend, but a wonderful colleague.

These are only two examples of how I learned the meaning of colleague. Certainly, for me, this is one of the many ingredients that makes a successful teaching career.

Going Further...

1. Do you remember your favorite teacher? Who was it and why was he/she your favorite?

CHAPTER 18

"A Spirit of Adventure"
Newfoundland

When I was just 7 years old, my dad was transferred to Pepperrell Air Force Base, in St. John's Newfoundland. We moved there during the summer between first and second grade, and lived there for 3 great years.

There is a point in Newfoundland, atop a high hill not far from its capital, St. John's, where you can stand at the easternmost part of North America. It is located in the Atlantic Ocean, miles from the mainland, and is one of the most beautiful places I have ever seen. I loved the time we spent there.

When we moved there, Newfoundland had no TV. We were used to having TV and wondered what we would do without it, but our family more than made up for it. We spent time together, sang together, played games together, and were always going somewhere. The people were some of the friendliest and most loving people I have ever met.

I have great memories of Newfoundland and all of the adventures it offered us. The island is truly a beauty of nature. We often took car rides in the country on Sunday mornings after church. The fields were full of wildflowers and there were hundreds of coves where you could stand and look out over the Atlantic. It was untouched, and the natural beauty inspired my 7-year-old self.

You could stand there and maybe see a school of whales, playing, as they dove in and out of the water. In the springtime you could find enormous icebergs from the north, melting and flowing in the warming waters. During the Second World War, Newfoundland was one of the northernmost outposts of protection for North America, and even today there are deserted forts with large rusting guns facing east, out into the beautiful, wild waters of the Atlantic. These sentinels of defense served us well then, and stand today as a memorial of all that occurred during those exciting, turbulent days of WWII. I loved to run around those forts and climb up and around the guns.

My mom would pack a picnic lunch often, and we would sit amidst the fields of wildflowers, enjoying the incredible blue skies and taking in the wonderful salty air. The smell of fish drying on racks in the small villages permeated the air as well on those wonderful sunny days.

It was quite an adventure for a young boy who dreamed of pirate ships attacking those coves, or whalers coming in to port. Each spring, the seal hunters visited St. John's Harbor. The sailors, mostly Portuguese, often came ashore with their booty, and I remember long processions with statues of the Virgin Mary, as they made their way to the cathedral to be blessed. I also remember spring days when the melting icebergs caused enormous chunks of ice to block the St. Johns harbor. A good view of that could be seen by climbing up the hill to Cabot Tower, named after the famous English sailor, John Cabot, and from which Marconi sent the very first wireless message. Talk about adventure! The island was resplendent, and remains embedded in my memory as one of the best parts of my childhood.

Many years later, my sister and I made a journey to the many places we had lived growing up, which included St. Johns. Being there felt like being home again, and I remembered so many of the places from 50 years ago. I heard the familiar sea chanties and ate cod tongue. I played on those guns at the forts, smelled the drying fish once again, and stood at the edge of a cliff, looking down at the blue Atlantic with the wind blowing in my face, soaking in the absolute beauty once more. I was reminded that memories are priceless, and need to be treasured. Newfoundland taught me to enjoy the adventuresome part of life and never fear trying something new and exciting.

Going Further...

1. Think about your favorite adventure. What was it? Where was it? When did it occur and how old were you?

2. There are two great movies (*Shipping News* and *Rare Birds*) which take place in Newfoundland. I have them in my collection and love to take them out once in a while to enjoy the beautiful scenery and to remember what a wonderful time of my life it was there. Check them out and you will see for yourself!

3. Try to listen to some of the fishing songs and other music of Newfoundland. You will hear many influences, such as the sea and the Irish heritage shared by the wonderful people of that exciting place.

CHAPTER 19

"Hope"
Holocaust Survivors

When I teach about the Holocaust or conduct a tour at our local Holocaust Museum, I often marvel to myself how people could have possibly managed to live through that incredibly horrible experience. I think of virtues like tenacity and bravery, and begin to understand. What amazes me most, especially when I hear them describe their harrowing and unbelievable stories, is that they all speak of hope.

Many lived through the loss of family and homes, ending up with absolutely nothing when it was over. They endured the horrific atrocities of madmen who considered it their destiny to deprive those innocent people of their very humanity, in order to create that "perfect" and exclusive society. You cannot listen to their recounting of what happened without crying, or being impressed and often swept away. And yet, it all comes down to one thing: they never lost hope.

Yes, for some, it was pure luck and even skill that helped them survive. For others, like Anne Frank and her family, it was the bravery of those who risked their lives to save and protect them. Denmark saved an incredible 7,200 Jewish lives in just 3 weeks, because they chose to be defiant and stand for what their King believed in: they were first and foremost, Danes.

Hope that there was a chance to see another day... hope that there would be freedom at last... hope that somehow, they could rise from the ashes of this terrible human tragedy of the 20th century to a new and better life.

I have been honored to meet many survivors and hear their stories. They have been there to encourage and inspire me to continue telling their story, and make sure that people remember. Helping them to remember what can happen when dislike turns to hatred, then murder, and other atrocities is important. The survivors keep me going, especially when I am criticized for exposing our children to these terrible things. They give me the strength and courage to tell their story and to teach young people about prejudice and discrimination, no matter how hard it is to hear. They give me determination to work towards the day when the word "hate" will no longer be in the dictionary.

It is possible from what I have learned from these Holocaust survivors. They have taught me to be an idealist and believe in a better world. They have given me hope that a day like that is not only possible, but not far off. As many of them get older and pass on, my promise to them is that I, and others, will not forget. Many thanks to you all! I love and appreciate you.

Going Further…

1. Go to the US Holocaust Memorial Museum's web site **https://www.ushmm.org** where you can find out what great things are being done by this incredible institution. Alternatively, find out if your community has a Holocaust Museum and a website.

    You will be able to hear for yourself some of the incredible personal testimonies of these great Holocaust survivors. You will get to know some true heroes.

CHAPTER 20

"True Happiness in Life"
Jagdish Davè

In the last few years of my teaching career, I met an extraordinary man one hot day in July. I was in Phoenix, Arizona, at a school similar to mine in Houston to attend a week-long institute. One of the topics was called "Wellness," and this man was there to teach us how to take care of ourselves as educators.

As we went around the room introducing ourselves, and this slight man from India began to talk about himself, I was astounded. I thought to myself, "there I am, 20 years from now." Jagdish was 83 years old, and as he spoke of his life and what had been important to him, I was truly amazed that he and I thought so much alike. For example, his professional life was dedicated to teaching, and he talked of what a great profession it was. He expressed a great love of young people and spoke of educating the whole child and having their interests at heart.

During the first few days of our classes, he spoke about coming to the realization, at an early age, that what he wanted to do most was teach. He also spoke of how difficult it was to bring himself to tell his parents that this is what he wanted to do, and then to break the news to them that he also wanted to go to the United States to teach.

He recalls the day he told his mother, and her reaction to his decision. As is the custom in some Asian cultures, he went to receive her blessing. He recalled that she placed her hands on his head to give him her blessing, reminding him that all that mattered was that he was going to do something that was his passion, and heart's desire. For her, that was all that mattered.

How long in my own teaching career had it taken me to come to that realization? It took leaving for a half dozen years to make me realize how much I missed it, and how important teaching was to me, but even more significant, how good a teacher I was. I knew when I returned to teaching that it was the only decision for me. I found, as Jagdish reminded us, that we had to find our "cup of tea." Once I did, I never looked back... I had no regrets. I knew I had the passion and talent to realize my potential to change the world by leading young minds and hearts to the truth found deep inside of them. This has been the great love in my professional life, and Jagdish Davè reinforced it, and truly moved me.

Jagdish emphasized that all of us must take care of ourselves, if we are to be of any value to those placed in our charge. He presented us with various stress relief and relaxation exercises from yoga which he freely admits are a vital part of his life. As a man well into retirement, he stated, "I retired the day I turned 20, when I began to do what I truly wanted, and what gave me life." It was not hard to see why he was as hearty and energetic as he was, with an attitude like that and attention to stress relief each day of his life.

In the desert of Arizona, I met a man late in my career, who truly gave me a great gift. He shared himself and his philosophy, and he showed me what matters most in anyone's life: that which truly gives us happiness.

Going Further...

1. In speaking to us in cups of tea, Jagdish Davè recommended his favorite book of recent years: "Three Cups of Tea". Ironically, I was reading it at that time, and I echo his recommendation... it is a good read.

2. Are you doing that which gives truly your life passion for living and satisfaction? Is there something you want to do someday, above everything else, in order to complete your life?

❧ CHAPTER 21 ❧

"Bravery and Sacrifice"
September 11, 2001

Today I think we lack true heroes for our young people to admire and emulate. Sure, there are definitely people they look up to, but the youth of today are faced with some pretty poor examples of "heroes." Young, professional ball players, earning exorbitant salaries, living a lifestyle that hardly qualifies as exemplary; musicians whose idea of "music" is reciting litanies directed against police, families, women, and using foul language; TV characters, especially men who come across as wimps and losers, again using foul language, and being put in their place by wise-guy kids. These are the types of "models" our young people have looked up to for too long.

Then, there was September 11, 2001. On that horrific day our young people saw for themselves what true bravery and sacrifice meant. Over 3,000 innocent citizens died that day for no explicable reason, except that hate was allowed to take control. On that awful day, the bright blue skies turned to acrid smoke and fire as we sat entranced, watching the incredible events of the day unfold. Our young people saw, along with the rest of us, how victory came out of sheer tragedy. The victory of bravery and sacrifice.

We saw the many brave firefighters, police, and public citizens who rushed forward putting themselves in danger to save others. Many lost their lives and became additional victims. We saw rescuer after rescuer exhibit Herculean efforts to help save those whose lives were forever changed on that pathetically sad day. Amidst our tears, we felt immense pride… pride that even in a moment of tragedy, our citizens could still muster up the effort to face horrific events with such bravery.

They became heroes to everyone, and showed our young people what true sacrifice really meant. Many were nameless to most of us, yet truly memorable. What a gift, a true gift. We can never forget them, what they did, and their valor.

Going Further...

1. Take a moment and keep silent for all those who lost their lives on that terrible day, in September of 2001.

2. What does "sacrifice" mean to you? How might it involve bravery? Talk to someone about that.

⸔ CHAPTER 22 ⸕

"Learning to Say Thank You"
Oprah W., Sam S., & Jesus

Thanksgiving has always been one of my favorite holidays. I have to admit that I suppose it is because I like to eat, especially a beautifully prepared Thanksgiving dinner. I love turkey and can eat it for days afterwards! I am glad that someone decided we should set aside one day each year to say thanks for everything that we have. That is another reason why I like Thanksgiving so much.

Pausing to be thankful is a great virtue to be cultivated, especially at the end of November, when the fall colors are at their peak and the air is crisp and clear. I like to reflect on how beautiful this holiday is. Truly American in all aspects, it reminds us never to take anyone or anything for granted, and to appreciate all we have. It is a reminder to take a moment and remember how fortunate we really are, whether thanking God for many un-merited gifts, or thanking others for all the favors and good things they do for us.

I love stories, and enjoy reading the parables of Jesus. One of my favorites is about his curing of the ten lepers, and the one who went back to say thanks. It reminds me how important a kind word of appreciation is, and it was evident in the story that even Jesus liked to be thanked. My lesson is clear: I am never too busy to be grateful and show it.

Oprah Winfrey has said that thankfulness is a virtue and we must work to cultivate it each day of our lives. She suggested that we thank God each day for 5 things we are grateful for. I have started my day that way for years noting 5 things I am thankful for. Sometimes, it is downright silly: peanut butter, a good pizza, last night's beautiful sunset, a great opera I saw, or white water rafting in Costa Rica. The many events and people in my life have been the subject of my daily prayer of thanks, and I am grateful to Oprah for introducing me to that great ritual, one which keeps me focused and humble at times.

I taught in a wonderful school, and every day I heard the words "thank you, Mr. Festa." After each class, more than one student turned to thank me as they left. After all those years in the classroom, I marveled that it still happened. I could be upset, chew them out, or even reprimand them, but when the period ended, some would still turn to say their thanks. It made me feel guilty at times.

One student who comes to mind is Sam Sands, truly one of the most polite and caring people I have met and had in my classroom. Sam and his family, brother Michael, mom Ellen Ann, and dad Mark, came to us in 2005 as refugees from Hurricane Katrina, in New Orleans. They had lost everything, and had moved in with relatives in Houston. They ended up at our school, with Sam in my 5th grade class. What a fine young man, and how wonderful it was to see his positive, happy go lucky attitude all the time. One thing I remember most about him was his gratitude. He always, and I mean ALWAYS, said thank you to me, sometimes several times a day. That is how I will always remember him. His brother was no different. I could tell they were a close-knit, loving family, deeply religious Orthodox Jews, and committed to each another. It showed in the way that both boys actively took part in many community service activities, and with helping others. Appreciation of all people is just one part of their character, and is something I have appreciated and enjoyed about them and several other students. Sam and Michael both went on to college, and I am certain that they are great successes.

Taking time to say thanks and showing appreciation is a vital part of what it takes to be a person of character. I am glad for these examples, and the many others from which I could learn.

Going Further...

1. What are you thankful for? Make a list. See how long it is.

2. Make it a point to say "Thank You" today to someone who would never expect it. Be specific in what you are thanking them for. See how it makes you (and them) feel!

CHAPTER 23

"The Importance of Family"
The Gaetas

In the Italian tradition, family is important. For an Italian, *la famiglia* is # 1, which I learned at an early age. My grandmother, Carmella Celtruda, lived with us when I was young, and I remember many Sunday afternoons when everyone would come to our place for dinner. It was like Christmas every time they came! I fondly recall my aunts, uncles, and cousins gathering there, and all the fun we had. They are memories I have carried with me through my life.

When I think of what it takes to be a great family, I think of the Gaeta family in Georgia. My cousin Joan Celtruda married Richard Gaeta in 1960. She was our oldest cousin, and the first one in our family to marry. They moved to Atlanta, Georgia some 15 years later, with 2 daughters and a son at the time, where they have remained to this day. A few more children, and several grandchildren have come along to complete this loving example of what it means to be a true family.

Joan and Richard believed strongly in the value of family and lived that during their entire marriage. They were close, and made it a point to keep in touch, whether they lived nearby or when some of them lived out of state. Today, they are all living in and around Atlanta.

Richard retired early, and he and Joan moved permanently to a house north of Atlanta to a small town named Hiawassee, on the banks of a lake. They remodeled their home to resemble a large Bed and Breakfast, named appropriately, "A la Famiglia" ("To the Family"). There was room to sleep countless grandchildren and children, and there were often as many as 20 or more there for a holiday celebration. I love the Gaetas. Their welcoming hospitality makes it so easy to love them, as they are generous with their kindness; there are no strangers in the Gaeta house.

One of their daughters, Theresa, moved to Houston with her husband, in order to start her own family. My daughter and I enjoyed having them there and we grew quite close to them. When they moved back to Georgia, we visited them a few times. I remember fondly, one particular Thanksgiving at the lake house. We were treated like royalty, and feasted heartily while we were there… there was much laughter and good times. I will never forget the wonderful boat ride with Richard on the "Fogettaboutit", and the great time we had talking about anything and everything. He was the kind of man you could always talk to easily. Several other visits there have shown me how much it means to stay close as a family, to accept each other, and be there for each other. When someone is with this family, it is evident there is a very strong bond, one that will never be broken. More people should see examples of loving families like this in our scattered, broken world, and they will see what dedication and commitment to each other can produce.

Tragically, in 2004, my cousin Joan contracted lung cancer, and instead of bringing down this family, they came together and bonded. Over a valiant 3-year battle, they were there for each other and with Joan in her brave struggle against this insidious disease. They educated themselves and others, joining her, and loving husband, Richard in enjoying every minute of her life, until her passing in July of 2007.

In characteristic fashion, they did not simply let Joan go, but committed themselves as a family to continue the fight against lung cancer. They established the Joan Gaeta Lung Cancer Foundation and are committed to raising public awareness, as well as funds, to fight this disease. In 2014 Richard died of cancer also, but to this day his children and grandchildren continue to remember their parents with great love and devotion. They have since sold the lake house but the memories remain. Memories of a family that exemplifies what it means to be *la famiglia*. I am proud and fortunate to call them family, and to have seen and shared firsthand their shining example of family values.

Going Further...

1. Go to "For Joan – Archive" at **http://gaetafund.org** to access information about the Joan Gaeta Lung Cancer Fund. Find out how you can learn more about lung cancer and be a part of this great work of the Gaeta family. Let them know you will not forget Joan and her legacy.

2. What memories do you have about your family that you would want to be sure were not forgotten?

❧ CHAPTER 24 ❧

"True Love of Others"
St. Teresa of Calcutta

If you were to ask friends of mine who my heroes are, for sure it would include Mother Teresa. From the moment I heard of her, I was sold on her general approach to people, especially her incredible, unselfish love for all who crossed her path.

I loved her story: growing up, not really knowing what to do with her life, experiencing a "conversion moment," then making a conscious decision to spend her life loving others, to a point that she literally gave her life for them. Not actually dying, but losing her own self to them.

I have read so much about her life, read and re-read her writings, and even purchased a CD once which featured songs based on her writings and talks. While watching a video about her life, I was struck by something she said, as she responded to a reporter's question about why she did what she did.

Mother Teresa recounted a time when she was walking the streets of Calcutta, as usual, seeking homeless and destitute people to feed and help in any way. She met a man... dirty, nearly naked, and lying in the filthy gutter of one of the crowded streets. He was barely breathing, and as she knelt down and cradled him in her arms, he looked up at her with powerful eyes. She began to clean his face, and in a weakened voice, he asked her very simply, "Why are you doing this? Why have you chosen me to help?"

Her answer to him, simple and brief, was a powerful statement of who this diminutive spark of life was, and how she fully lived her life. To answer his question, she simply said "because I love you". For me, this is true love of others without any strings attached. Unconditional.

Mother Teresa became world famous, winning the Nobel Peace Prize and having her photo taken with many world leaders. Yet, she never lost her intense, genuine love and care for others, always putting them first, especially the poor and those forgotten by society.

She is one of my heroes, who has set a good example of what true Christian love is, and has been a role model for me since her death in 1997. She was canonized a Catholic saint by Pope Francis in 2016.

Going Further...

1. Read some of Mother Teresa's writings. Take your time and ponder the words. Let them sink in and reflect on how they apply to your life.

2. Read a biography of this incredible woman.

3. Find out more about the Co-Workers of Teresa. Although not an organization, they form a family around the world and assist Mother Teresa's order, the Missionaries of Charity. Contact them to find out more:

> Co-Workers of Mother Teresa
> 8 Stardust Drive
> Sherman, Illinois 62684

CHAPTER 25

"Standing Up for Justice"
Archbishop Oscar Romero

One summer, in 2002, I stood at a very important place, for me personally. It was on the exact spot where on a morning in March of 1980, Oscar Romero, Archbishop of El Salvador, was assassinated while saying Mass.

I was in El Salvador to study the effect of the Catholic Church in the life of the people of that war-ravaged poverty-stricken country. It was important that I be there to see where one of my true heroes had walked, and had eventually given his life for the principles he believed in.

Oscar Romero was a talented young man when he was ordained a priest. He was sent to Rome to study and was considered a "rising star" in the Salvadoran Church. And, indeed, he was. He rose quickly through the ranks of the clergy and became a bishop.

Later, he was asked to take on the role of Archbishop, the head of the entire Church in El Salvador. He had been involved in priestly work for many years, and it seemed, when looking at his life, that he was part of the establishment, and did little to improve the lot of his people.

The country has always been extremely poor and unstable. At the time of Romero's rise to the position of Archbishop, the country was embroiled in a great civil war which brought on great misery. Countless innocent people lost their lives, and many more were assassinated for being suspected of supporting the rebel cause against the government. It was in that atmosphere that Oscar Romero experienced, I believe, a real conversion.

He loved his people, but when put in the position of national leadership in the Church, he truly took on the people's cause and began to speak out loudly against the terrible abuses and degradation of his people. Day after day, he criticized the government that caused so much suffering in his beloved country.

Slowly, what developed in him was a true vision of love and service towards the poor and suffering. Oscar Romero became the voice of the people of El Salvador. As more people were ruthlessly killed, like his good friend Rutilio Grande, American nuns, and the Jesuits massacred at their own university, Romero called on his countrymen who were part of the government's army to lay down their arms. In a famous sermon, shortly before his death, he commanded all the soldiers in the cathedral to lay down their arms in the name of Jesus Christ. Certainly, threatening words, and words which sealed his fate.

Oscar Romero called his people to a more genuine relationship with their God, emphasizing what is known as the "option for the poor." He was clear and precise about what the Christian commitment meant, and it was obvious that he was even willing to give his own life for those principles. He stood up for what was right and did not falter. On the very day that an assassin came to the chapel where he was celebrating Mass, he had preached the following words, a testimony to the dedication and love he had for all people. These were his last words uttered in public, for as he finished the homily, he was gunned down in cold blood.

> *"God's reign is already present in our earthly mystery. When the Lord comes, it will be brought to perfection. (from "The Church in the Modern World", Vatican Council II)*
>
> *That is the hope that inspires Christians. We know that every effort to better society, especially when injustice and sin are so ingrained, is an effort that God blesses, that wants, that God demands of us."*

Oscar Romero was considered a saint by his countrymen immediately following his death. Until the papacy of Francis, the Catholic Church did very little to make his sainthood official. Perhaps he was too controversial, taking a stand that might have been embarrassing, or politically incorrect at the time for the Church's hierarchy in El Salvador and Rome. What always impressed me was that he did the right thing by taking a stand. He was so convinced it was the right thing to do, that he was willing to give his very life to make it meaningful. For that, I love and admire him, and like scores of so many of his countrymen today I have always considered him a real saint, an example for all of us of what it means to be a true Christian.

Oscar Romero was finally recognized for his work and life by the Catholic Church when Pope Francis canonized him a saint in 2018.

Going Further...

1. There are two excellent movies about Oscar Romero: "Salvador" and "Romero". I recommend them both. They give distinctly different views of that time in war-ravaged El Salvador. The writing and acting are superb, and I am always moved whenever I watch them again.

2. Many true gems form Romero's pen, his speeches and homilies have been assembled in a wonderful publication called: *The Violence of Love: The Pastoral Wisdom of Archbishop Oscar Romero*. James Brockman, S.J., an expert in the life and writings of Romero, has done a great job, and each page is filled with something to read and contemplate. It gives one a true picture of the man Oscar Romero became, and his beautiful dedication to the Catholic religion. This is a great read!

CHAPTER 26

"Being a Great Teacher"
John "Jack" Carr

In the fall of 1970, my first year of teaching, I registered to take a dreaded education course at the University of Maryland. My intention was to begin the state teacher certification process. My teaching career, however, started in a private, "independent" school. I was hired without the certification. As a matter of fact, in all my years in the classroom, I have never been required to have a teaching license, or go through the long process to be certified and maintain that honorable distinction. In addition to awards, I have also had the confidence and praise of students, parents, and administrators. I owe much of my success in the classroom to one person who got me off to a good start.

That was John "Jack" Carr, my teacher for that first education class. He came in on day one, threw a book down on the desk and told us this was the required text. We could read it if we wanted to, (a book he incidentally co-authored). But the book he really wanted to require us to read was "Teaching as a Subversive Activity", by Postman and Weingarten. When I got that paperback, I should have had an inkling of what it would be: there was a picture of an apple on the cover, made to look like a bomb about to go off. That book, and Jack Carr's wonderful lectures set me on a road which would lead to excellence in the profession I was choosing.

I learned some valuable 'lessons' that semester when I would finish teaching and travel far to the University of Maryland Campus. I think that was the most important course I had ever taken. One of the first chapters in the book he asked us to read is called, "Crap Detecting", and that probably gave me the direction I needed. Jack Carr told us the most important thing we had to do as educators was to prepare our students for their retirement: what life skills would we be teaching them, no matter our field, that would help them to deal with all the leisure time they would have one day. He predicted that as the century turned in 30 years, people would, indeed, have more leisure time. He was right. We may seem busier, but we sure play a lot.

Jack Carr gave me the basics of what would become my teaching philosophy, which has not changed much over the decades: The students come first, no matter what... their interests are paramount. Over the years, I have come to realize that it is not just my presence in the classroom which makes a difference, but my presence in their lives. I have challenged them to make a difference in the world as they pass through. That is what I want to do. I have seen just how important my presence in their lives has been, and often I asked myself, did I show compassion? Did I give them attention? Was I a good listener, and an advocate for them? These were the things that came to mean something, not the material I asked them to regurgitate. That was something anyone could do, but to change enough to become an agent of change one day, I realized that I would have a lot to do with that attitude.

As the years went by, I realized how important my students would be in the next century, in a world that was becoming more diversified, complicated, impersonal, and self-centered. They would have many challenges as the 20th century became the 21st, and I was a vital part of who and what they would become. How will they handle it? Jack Carr had the answer.

Jack told us to get to know them, so they would not just be strangers sitting in front of us each day. He told us to listen to their music, read their magazines, and watch their movies and TV shows, which I did, as hard as it was at times. I became a fan of Yoda, followed Harry Potter in his adventures, listened to Smashing Pumpkins, Hannah Montana, and even rap music. I have read Twilight and the Alex Ryder books, watched The Simpsons and Family Guy. I was able to talk about what I did, and seemed to relate to them, because I showed them that THEY were important to me. Coming out of that has been a wonderful experience. I shared many books with my students and encouraged them to read some incredible young adult fiction.

In the movie Field of Dreams, we are told, "If you build it, they will come." In my classroom, I feel that is what I have done: I created a place where they could be themselves and grow as a person... a place where they could be accepted and respected for who they were. Indeed, they did come, and some have "stayed." As each school year began, I always pointed to an aging sign on the wall. It had one word on it: RESPECT. Referring to Aretha Franklin's song with the same name, I always told my students that was the key to success in my classroom: mutual respect. I for them, and they for me. And I never let them forget that all year.

Thank you, Jack Carr, for pointing me in the right direction; a direction from which I hardly deviated; a direction which I hope has touched the lives of hundreds; and, a direction which has made me who I am today as a retired educator.

Going Further...

1. Did you ever have a teacher who you remember advocated for you? What moment(s) do you remember?

2. What "crap detecting" do you remember from your school days?

3. If you have not done so already, call, text, or write to a former teacher of yours and thank him/her for being there for you. Do it today!

CHAPTER 27

"The Value of True Friendship"
Elizabeth "Bette" Breaz

I would have to say that one of my truest and best friends has been Elizabeth "Bette" Breaz. We first met at a support group for divorced and widowed people at our parish, and have developed a close friendship over the past 35 years. She has taught me so much about what it means to be a good friend.

She was, as I found out, a real "organizer", as well as a true people person. Bette never meets the proverbial stranger. She has great instincts for seeking out a person who needs a good friend at a particular moment, and is always willing to invite anyone into her life. She really exemplifies what "friend" means.

Our close relationship began when I was attending graduate school part time to get a Master's degree in Counseling Psychology. I had a problem finding child care, being a single dad at that time. Classes at the university went from 4:30 - 8:00 PM. One week I was in a panic. My usual child care plans had fallen through, and I had no one to care for my daughter. Bette found out and volunteered to help me... something she did extremely well. She then began caring for my daughter every week, by adjusting her own volunteer schedule at a local food bank. She picked up my daughter from school and watched her until I was free, often feeding her dinner and helping with homework. Thus, a true friendship began.

Over the years, I've seen how Bette interacts with everyone she meets. She becomes their friend, no matter how old or young, where they are from, or their personal situation. Everyone is Bette's friend from the moment she meets them.

She is always the first to volunteer for a project and is great about getting others to join in. She is, as one can guess, very outgoing, positive, and caring.

We have become part of each other's lives, celebrating both the happy and sad moments together. I have celebrated holidays with Bette and her close-knit family and truly feel a warm connection to them. I know and love each of her children and grandchildren. For me, they are like my own family. In fact, she is "Buna" to my grandchildren.

"Buna" is the Romanian word for grandmother. Bette is very proud of her Romanian heritage, and shares it with anyone who will listen. I was blessed to meet the original "Buna," Bette's dear mother. She was a truly unique individual, and after meeting her and getting to know her it was not hard to see why Bette is the wonderful woman she is today. "Buna" was one of those rare human beings who instantly touched you with her love and dedication. Bette's loving and giving nature had come from growing up with Buna's teachings.

In one's life, it is likely we will have only a few "best friends", and rarer to have such a good friend for so long. How blessed I am to have been able to learn about true friendship from my best friend, Bette Breaz.

Bette "Buna" Breaz, died peacefully on Thanksgiving Day, 2020, just three days after her 91st birthday. When her daughter Vickie called to tell me she was in hospice, my son-in-law Nathan and I drove to Houston just to see her and say good-bye, returning home that same afternoon. Her congestive heart failure had slowly taken over, and it was difficult to know if she was fully cognizant. When I leaned over to kiss her on the cheek and told her who it was, she opened her eyes, looked at me, smiled and said: "We did have some good times together, didn't we?" We sure did Bette! I wrote this before Bette died, and I chose to leave it in the present tense. She is gone, but still a viable presence in my life.

Going Further...

1. Bette has exemplified this quote from Camus for me:

   Don't walk in front of me, I may not follow.
   Don't walk behind me, I may not lead.
   Walk beside me and just be my friend.

   Who has done that for you in your life?

2. How do you celebrate *your* ethnicity? What have your relatives shared with you about where you have come from?

3. Write a note to a good friend, telling her/him how much you appreciate their friendship. Do it today!

CHAPTER 28

"Taking Life Too Seriously"
The Indispensable Man

Sometime when you're feeling important,
Sometime, when your ego's in bloom
Sometime, when you take it for granted,
You're the best qualified in the room

Sometime, when you feel that you going
Would leave an unfillable hole,
Just follow this simple instruction
And see how it humbles your soul.

Take a bucket and fill it with water;
Put your hand in it, up to the wrist;
Pull it out, and the hole that's remaining
Is a measure of how you'll be missed.

You may splash all you please when you enter;
You can stir up the water galore;
But stop, and you'll find in a minute
That it looks quite the same as before.

The moral in this quaint example
Is to do just the best that you can,
Be proud of yourself, but remember,
There's no indispensable man!

This bit of advice was on the wall of my classrooms for years. I was blessed to teach many truly talented and motivated kids in my career. It was rare to encounter a "bad" student. My students have known success and hard work, and I believe they have benefited from it. When you live a blessed life, it is easy to do two things:

1. Take ourselves too seriously.

2. Take things for granted.

The Indispensable Man has taught me to remember these two points every day. As I begin each day, I like to give thanks for what I have. I try to remember that it is not only my hard work, but sometimes also pure chance which has blessed my life with so many wonderful people and events. Each moment I have allows me to be grateful, and to remember that all of this is merely temporary. Everything can be gone in a flash... so I try to savor each and every moment. I want to enjoy my life, and get what I can out of it. Most importantly, I have tried to make a positive difference in my world.

To do that successfully, I believe that each of us has to have a sensible perspective of life, and realize that the world does not revolve around ME! This is what I have tried to instill in my students when I tell them not to take themselves too seriously.

When I was in college, I worked one summer as the manger of a swimming pool. Something happened to my car, and I remember feeling frustrated and venting to my dad about what would happen if I did not make it to the pool in time to open it. His comment to me, though appearing cold and indifferent, had a lot of wisdom in it: "So what happens," he asked me, "if today you drop dead? You think the pool won't open tomorrow without you?" It made me think, and I began to realize at a young age what it means to take ourselves too seriously.

I am a big fan of playtime. In a competitive, hard-working environment it is easy to be so intensely focused on our goal, and/or target project, that we forget to take the time to just be ourselves: to rest, to relax, and to play! This is how I remember not to take myself too seriously. For many "type-A" personalities this can be a difficult thing to commit to, remembering not to take oneself too seriously.

That hole in the water imagery from the above poem is a sobering one. But it is also an invitation to be myself, and to remember the child within who wants to play once in a while.

Going Further…

1. How do you play? Where? When?

2. When have you been particularly proud of an accomplishment? Explain.

3. How about a time when you failed? What happened? Why?

❧ CHAPTER 29 ☙

"Dreaming Your Dream"
Rev. Dr. Martin Luther King, Jr.

"Work hard, play hard, dream hard, and you can make your dreams come true." (Anonymous)

When we are young, we have dreams. "What do you want to be when you grow up?" We think about the future a lot as we grow up. Choosing a college major is all about that, and all that thinking is not devoid of a few dreams.

Martin Luther King, like many other visionaries (Gandhi, Paul McCartney, Jesus Christ, to name a few), imagined a world of peace and justice. He was not afraid to speak about his dream and work hard to make it a reality. In doing so, he confronted incredible odds: hatred, bigotry, violence, personal attacks, imprisonment, and even death. And yet, he never shrank from any of that, so dedicated was he to his cause. Today he is considered a role model, and a success.

On a hot afternoon in Washington, D.C. in the month of August in 1963, he stood at the Lincoln Memorial on the Mall and delivered his now famous "I Have a Dream" speech. Thousands of young children have read it, and memorized it. At the time, I was only 18 years old, and with some close African American friends of our family I watched him deliver his speech live on television. To be honest, I hardly understood it and had only a vague idea of what was going on. As I grew older, I began to understand what it meant to have a dream, and how to work to make it become a reality.

It was April, 1968, just 5 years later that I really understood the message. That evening when I heard the news of MLK's death, I feel I underwent a great change. I was barely an adult in those dark days which followed his assassination, but it was then that I began to realize that it was not the end of his dream… it was just the beginning. The beginning of my adult life in which I would teach others about dreams and hopes, and our call to make them all come true, no matter the cost.

It was on that April night when the seeds of this book were planted, though it would not come to light for many more years. In the years that followed I have been challenged, both in and out of the classroom, about why I do what I do, and to support what I have. Whether teaching the lessons of the Holocaust, making my school a "No Place for Hate" institution, or preaching and teaching about social justice, I have found myself encouraging other people to dream. I want them to imagine a world where love is the norm, where hatred is a thing of the past, where justice is the common denominator, and peace is something that all people can truly know and experience.

I think this all came into focus for me one day many years ago, when an anonymous 7th grader came by my room after school to talk. He asked me if I thought all this "stuff" I taught about in class really made a difference. He totally caught me off guard, and I had to mentally scramble for a good answer. In an instant, I was "enlightened" enough to say to him: "If only one of you hears me and decides to make a difference in the world today by making it a better place to be, then I know I will have been a success." I was silently congratulating myself and patting myself on the back, for coming up with something so clever, so quickly. I was even astounded by my apparent brilliance! But then, he said something as only a 13-year-old boy could, which truly put it all in the right perspective. "Oh," he told me. "I get it." He got it! Yes, maybe that year he was the one I touched. He was the one who would take my words and lessons to heart and begin to change the world, to make dreams come true.

For me, this is what making dreams come true is all about. And I think Martin Luther King, Jr. knew that!

Going Further…

1. What is one of your dreams? Talk about it.

2. *"Hope for tomorrow thrives in our dreams." (Anonymous)*
   What can you do to make Martin Luther King Jr.'s dream come true?

3. A delightful little book you can get to think more about dreams is called, "Follow Your Dreams". It is a collection of thoughts and quotes about and for dreamers. They have been compiled by Liesel Vazquez, and published by Peter Pauper Press, Inc., White Plains, New York.

CHAPTER 30

"Priorities"
St. Francis of Assisi

Since I was a teenager, the Prayer of St. Francis has been something I have read and re-read. I have tried to use it as a compass for my entire life. One summer, as I walked the streets of Assisi, Italy, I felt a true connection with this incredible person who has been such a guiding light for me. The words of his Prayer have always been a true inspiration:

Lord, make me an instrument of your peace;
Where there is hatred, let me sow love;
Where there is injury, pardon;
Where there is doubt, faith;
Where there is despair, hope;
Where there is darkness, light;
Where there is darkness, light;
Where there is sadness, joy.

O Divine Master, grant that I may seek not so much to be consoled, as to console; to be understood, as to understand; to be loved, as to love; for it is in giving that we receive; it is in pardoning that we are pardoned, and it is in dying that we are born to Eternal Life.

I have always loved Francis' story. He was born into a wealthy 13th century family, and gave it all up. It is said that he saw a leper on the road, and that the sight of this terribly ill man caused him to flee. Later, he is said to have undergone a complete conversion and to have turned his life around, setting before him the true priority of life: the welfare of others. He led a life full of service to others, and started an order of brothers, and then nuns, whose only work was to serve others.

Francis has been accorded great honor from the Catholic Church, to be called a saint, but in reality, he like so many other true saints, would most likely turn away from such adulation. His life showed us that he would have likely believed strongly in the old adage "actions speak louder than words," because he is reputed to have said: "Preach at all times; use words, if necessary."

The greatest direction I have received from St. Francis is to act, rather than talk. I believe this world would be a better place if more of us would stop discussing and debating, and just roll up our sleeves and get to work. It must be about the work of saving this world in so many ways, and Francis's call to action provides the kind of example we need: what should be our true priority in life?

Going Further...

1. What are your priorities?

2. What do you think is the biggest challenge facing the human race today?

3. How can we be true peacemakers, in the style of Francis of Assisi?

CHAPTER 31

"Faith in Action"
Catholic Relief Services

Five years after I retired, I heard a speaker talk about an organization I had heard of before, but knew very little about, Catholic Relief Services. Founded in 1943 during World War II, it is an international humanitarian organization working daily to end poverty, hunger, and disease worldwide, serving millions of people each year.

During that talk, I discovered that Catholic Relief Services ("CRS") had a program which prepared deacons and priests to speak and preach about social action in the Catholic Church through CRS. I researched that program, called Global Fellows, and was chosen when I applied. With some preparation, I began to seek opportunities to tell people about the great work of CRS. Their motto is: "Faith. Action. Results." Wherever there is a problem in the world, CRS attempts to be there to offer help and assistance in the areas of Emergency Response and Recovery, Agricultural Livelihoods, and Health and Social Services.

Working with CRS, I have met an incredible number of professionals, both here in the U.S., and abroad, who work tirelessly to make this organization one of the most efficient aid organizations in the world. I have learned much from these people and their work: dedication, hard work, care, compassion, and adherence to the Gospel values of peace and justice.

In January 2019, I was invited to make a week's trip to Uganda as part of my formation to see CRS in action. While there, I experienced firsthand the results of the many programs having to do with family education, health and sanitation, education, and refugee relief. I visited one of the world's largest refugee settlements in northwest Uganda, and saw for myself the utter devastation and misery of those who have fled their own countries, the immigrants we hear so much about. It was there that I met a man named Charles, who had fled his own country with his family to be safe and survive, only to lose his entire family along the way. He arrived at the refugee camp alone, with nothing, and yet, when I met him, he was volunteering as a translator for those who were in his same situation. He told me he was doing it to give back for all that he had received from CRS. He was a true disciple.

Each year during Lent, CRS sponsors the Rice Bowl program to provide a valuable resource and a way to become familiar with CRS and all it does. I am always happy to speak about it, and distribute the Rice Bowls to as many people as I can.

CRS has been a vital part of my life these past few years, and has shown me that faith is not just something you talk about or "feel." It is action… action to make the world a better place.

Going Further…

1. Go to **http://crs.org** and find out more about Catholic Relief Services. Watch their videos, and read about the incredible work this organization is doing.

2. There are many ways to help CRS in its work, and to become involved in worthwhile projects. Choose something that you can do to be a part of the CRS family.

CHAPTER 32

"Appreciating All Life's Gifts"
All Those Not Mentioned

Over the years, many people and events have touched me and made me who I am today. In the preceding pages, I have written about many people, but surely not all who have contributed to my life story. There are countless others of you who have touched me, and made an impression in some way.

Like those in the stories and anecdotes you have just read, you, too, have made a difference, because in your own way, you have made an impression on me. You may have passed by, hardly taking notice nor interacting, but rest assured, you have made a difference. Others of you have played a big part in the past years of my life. Your impact has been felt and appreciated, and I tell you, it has been important.

There's a story I've heard, probably anonymous like so many others, which seems to help me express my thanks to all of you, mentioned or not, here in these pages.

Many centuries ago, a small boy is said to have passed by a man working in front of his shop. He was a sculptor, chiseling away at a large block of marble. The boy was mesmerized, watching him for a long period of time in awe, soon tiring, however, and moving on.

A few days later, the young boy passed by the sculptor again and stopped to watch him work on the same piece of marble. Imagine the boy's surprise when instead of seeing a large, plain block of marble, he saw a beautiful, magnificent statue of a mighty lion. After watching the artist at work for a period of time, he finally spoke to him, saying: "How did you know there was a lion inside of that big block of stone?"

Yes, how did he know? My point? Simple. I am grateful to all who have entered my life, at any point, to help me realize my potential, to make me who I am. Behind the scenes or actively involved, I appreciate all who have helped me to discover the lion within me. Thank you.

Going Further...

1. Michelangelo, the famous artist, received a compliment once about the carving of an angel that he had completed. His comment, was similar to the story you just read above: "I saw the angel in the marble and I carved until I set him free."

   Who has been your sculptor in life, setting you free to be who you are, letting God do his work?

2. Whom have you helped to discover their lion within?

3. If you wish, let me know how you liked this book, and what these stories have meant to you.

   You can contact me at: **atsef@aol.com**

༆ EPILOGUE ༆

Once, many years ago, I was teaching a high school class about death and the next life. I asked the students to do an interesting activity: draw their own tombstone with an epitaph they would like people to remember them by one day.

They asked me to do one, and once I got over the weird feeling of having to do it, I made one. As I was completing the project, and actually writing the words on my hand drawn tombstone, I had to think hard. What would I want to leave behind when I am gone? What would I want people to remember me for? You can probably imagine that I had many ideas! But, suddenly, two words came to mind. Two words which seemed to be most appropriate for my tombstone. And years later, I have not changed my mind.

"He tried"... that's all I can really say about anything I have ever done. I tried. I made an effort. Yoda, from the Star Wars movies, another of my favorites and a source of wisdom for me, said: "There is no try, only do". I still believe that before I can *do* anything, I have to make an effort to *try*. Trying begets doing.

I tried to be the best son, brother, dad, friend, grandfather, teacher, minister, volunteer, etc., that I could ever be. And now, as I look back, my heart is full of love and appreciation for all who have opened up their hearts, minds and lives to share something to help me try to be the best person I can be. This, for me, is the ultimate happiness.

My headstone will be very simple: my name, my dates and the following two words:

"He Tried"

Image Credits

Front cover photograph by Balaji Srinivasan
Title: "Grayscale Photo of a Hallway"
Usage permitted via Pexels License

Rear cover photograph by Emre Can Acer
Title: "French Doors Slightly Opened"
Usage permitted via Pexels License

All other images used with permission via Pexels License

Known Photographers include:

Hisham Yahya (pg. 14)
Oleg Magni (pg. 17)
Julia Volk (pg. 40)
Rafael Albaladejo (pg. 51)
Rajesh Kumar Verma (pg. 57)
Tetyana Kovyrina (pg. 60)
Craig Adderley (pg. 77)
Jad El Mourad (pg. 88)

www.ingramcontent.com/pod-product-compliance
Lightning Source LLC
Chambersburg PA
CBHW030111240426
43673CB00002B/43

9781956845037